Passive Income Mastery

Strategies for Entrepreneurs and Solopreneurs

by

Ethan J. Sterling

Passive Income Mastery:

Strategies for Entrepreneurs and Solopreneurs

Table of Contents

Introduction

Unveiling the Power of Passive Income

Imagine a life where you earn money as you sleep, where your earnings are not shackled by the hours you can physically work. Let's unwrap this alluring idea of making your assets work for you rather than you work tirelessly for them. It's not mere wishful thinking; it's the powerful realm of passive income.

Now, we live in a fast-paced world where the gig economy, side hustles, and the entrepreneurial spirit are flourishing more than ever. Amidst this dynamic landscape, mastering the art of passive income has become not just an advantage but a necessity for those wanting to outpace the competition and secure their financial future.

I see you — the entrepreneur with a vision, the blogger crafting stories, the individual yearning for a side hustle that stands the test of time. You're seeking the golden goose of income generation, and you're in the right place. This book is an invitation to ignite your income stream without proportionately increasing your workload.

Let's start by debunking a common myth: Passive income isn't about getting something for nothing. It's about smart strategies, a bit of upfront effort, followed by continuous tweaking to maintain a steady flow of income. It's a promise of financial gains, potentially significant, through avenues that, after initial legwork, demand less of your direct involvement.

The chapters laid out before you are a roadmap. They will lead you through the foundations, into the burgeoning world of affiliate marketing, onto content creation, and right up to maximizing your online presence. We'll explore engaging your audience, scaling with automation, and overcoming the pitfalls that inevitably arise.

Throughout these pages, we won't just skim the surface. You'll tap into actionable strategies that are designed to build a sturdy, sustainable passive income stream. It will be a deep dive into the world of passive wealth-building, tailored for your entrepreneurial mindset and zest for growth.

The strategies covered here are not about creating a quick buck, nor are they pie-in-the-sky theories. They're proven tactics that have worked for countless entrepreneurs before you. These are comprehensive methods, broken down into manageable steps, to help you build a passive income fortress brick by brick.

I want you to envision your future, one where the stress of living paycheck to paycheck becomes a distant memory. Picture a life where you have the freedom to pursue your passions because your financial health isn't wholly dependent on trading your time for money.

But with great freedom comes great responsibility. This book calls on you to act, to apply what you learn, and to stand firm against the allure of complacency. The passive income streams you will cultivate are akin to nurturing a garden — they need care, attention, and an understanding of the ecosystem in which they thrive.

We'll steer clear of get-rich-quick illusions and focus on substantial and ethical income generation. Together, we'll pull back the curtain on the methods that can supplement or even replace traditional earnings with ongoing revenue streams that bolster your financial stability.

Brace yourself for inspiration infused with a healthy dose of pragmatism. We're setting out to ignite that fire in your belly, the one that's fueled by autonomy and the pursuit of a life less ordinary. The journey ahead is for the bold, the committed, for you who are not just dreamers but doers.

Take a moment to fasten your mental seatbelt — not to brace for a jarring ride, but for a journey to financial independence that is about to take off. You're not just reading a book; you're stepping onto a path lined with the potential for growth, personal freedom, and the sweet savor of earned success.

Your goals are achievable. The strategies within these chapters are your tools, and this introduction is your launch pad. Together, we will unveil and harness the power of passive income. Let's turn that vision of financial success into your living, breathing reality.

Chapter 1

Foundations of Passive Income

Imagine a life where your financial growth isn't tethered to the clock, where earnings flow whether you're typing away at your desk or sipping a latte in a sun-drenched cafe. That's the beauty of passive income—the foundation upon which dreams of financial freedom are built. To begin with, it's essential to understand that passive income isn't a mythical beast; it's real, attainable, and right within your grasp if you play your cards right. This chapter will uncomplicate the complexities of passive income streams, showing you that there's more to it than just hoping for a windfall. You'll discover that your unique skills and experiences are keys to unlocking a world where income doesn't stop when you do. By tapping into your inherent potential, you're not just earning, you're crafting a legacy that operates like a well-oiled machine, humming to the rhythm of your life's design. Dive in, and let's explore the foundational elements that can propel you from a cycle of active pursuit to the echelons of entrepreneurial enlightenment, where earning is not merely an act, but an art.

Understanding Passive Income Streams

For the hustlers out there spinning multiple plates and the bloggers tirelessly curating content, grasping the essence of passive income streams is akin to discovering buried treasure. It's the holy grail of financial freedom, offering income potential that isn't directly tied to the hours worked. But what exactly does this involve, and how can you, as an entrepreneur or solopreneur, dive into these waters?

Firstly, let's get one thing straight: passive income isn't about getting rich quickly. It's about strategically investing time, resources, or money upfront to create a system that generates income without requiring constant hands-on effort. Think of it like planting a garden. You select the seeds (the investment), cultivate the soil (set up the system), and over time, with a bit of maintenance, you enjoy a fruitful yield.

From real estate investments where properties are rented out, to creating digital products that sell around the clock, the beauty of passive income lies in its diversity. A blogger might monetize their content with affiliate marketing, where they earn a commission every time a reader purchases through their link. This income stream would be coming in whether that blogger is tapping away at their keyboard or sipping coffee in a Parisian café.

Now, don't be fooled; the 'passive' in passive income can be a bit of a misnomer. Initially, there's nothing passive about it. It demands vision, grit, and tenacity to build. It's like constructing a machine piece by piece. Once it's assembled and running smoothly, only then does the automation aspect kick in, and the passive part of the narrative truly begins.

This is where clarity becomes crucial. Distinguishing between the types of passive income is key to understanding where your efforts should be directed. Some streams are product-based, like writing an eBook or developing an app. Others hinge on investment, where capital is employed to buy stocks or cryptocurrency that appreciates over time without much interference. Then there are those that rely on advertising revenue, like YouTube channels or blogs that pull in money from the ads displayed on their high-traffic sites.

But to simply float on autopilot without a care? That's not how winners are shaped. Managing and perfecting your income streams is part of the groundwork. It's about fine-tuning that sales funnel, tweaking your ad strategies, or refreshing that evergreen content to keep it relevant. Passive? Somewhat. Hands-off? Rarely. The goal is to shift the scale from active to passive over time.

Beyond the first setup, passive income endeavors often call for a period of nurturing. Affiliate marketing efforts might start with you actively pitching products. However, once the SEO is dialed in and your site ranks, your content begins to pull in traffic and sales with little to no daily effort. The crucial aspect here is ensuring the passive income stream aligns with your niche, your passion, or your skill set. When these align, the effort doesn't feel so burdensome.

Importantly, risk management mustn't be ignored. While it's tempting to throw all your energy into one passive income stream that seems promising, diversification is your safety net. Just like in investing, spreading your avenues of passive income can help cushion against unforeseen market shifts or changes in consumer behavior. If one stream meets a drought, others can continue to flow.

And let's talk about scalability. That's the beauty of many passive income models – they can often be scaled up without a linear increase in effort. For instance, an online course can be sold to ten students or ten thousand, with the same foundational content. The infrastructure to scale these models is often built within digital space, using global reach and technology.

Transitioning to a passive income mindset also requires a shift in time management. It's about prioritizing tasks that construct or enhance your income-generating assets further, rather than those that offer immediate but finite payoffs. As you navigate this landscape, you'll learn to discern where your time yields the highest returns, quite literally.

For the solopreneurs and bloggers, the rise in creator platforms has opened a plethora of avenues for passive income. You can automate the distribution and sale of creative work, from templates to online courses, without moving a muscle once everything is set up. Platforms take care of transactional coordination, leaving creators to focus on what they do best – creating.

Moreover, passive income streams often have a cumulative effect. Initial success breeds more success, and as your brand and reputation grow, so do your earnings. The algorithms of platforms like YouTube favor channels with higher engagement, which further boosts visibility and revenue – a virtuous cycle that helps those who've done the groundwork.

Now, embarking on the journey to set up passive income streams isn't without its challenges. It requires a balance of creativity, strategic planning, and, yes, patience. It's more akin to a chess game than a slot machine. Each move should be calculated and aimed at positioning you towards eventual financial autonomy.

In essence, understanding passive income streams is more than recognizing opportunities. It's about constructing a life raft with the right materials so that when the tide of active work recedes, you're not left stranded. It's crafting the kind of future where your income is not shackled to the finite hours of the day. This chapter illuminates that path, setting you on course to wield your talents in a way that ensures they keep adding value – and cash to your bank account – even while you sleep.

Identifying Your Passive Income Potential

As we pivot from understanding what passive income streams are all about, let's turn our focus to a critical aspect – recognizing the potential within you for generating passive income. Navigating this entrepreneurial terrain requires a good look at what you've got to offer, coupled with a reality check of what's achievable. Here's the good news – whether you're a tenacious entrepreneur, a creative blogger, or someone hunting for that lucrative side hustle, you've got a treasury of passive income opportunities waiting to be unlocked.

First off, let's get real. Passive income doesn't magically happen overnight. It's the result of strategic planning and consistent effort. Think about your skills, interests, and the value you can provide to others. This reflection isn't about erecting castles in the sky, it's about laying down solid ground for potential income streams to flourish.

Are you a wordsmith with a knack for captivating stories? Blogging could be your goldmine. Translate those narratives into e-books or create an online course teaching others your literary prowess. For the tech-savvy, developing an app or software tool that solves a frequent problem can be your ticket to recurring revenue.

Picture your biggest strengths. What do you excel at without breaking a sweat? Your passive income venture should align with your core competencies. Capitalize on your existing knowledge and ability. If you're a whiz at web design, consider creating templates or tutorials. Your prowess can help others build their digital empire, all while padding your wallet.

Market needs are like the compass that should guide your passive income journey. Savvy entrepreneurs keep their fingers on the pulse of market trends. What are folks clamoring for? What's that pressing need or pain point that you can alleviate? When you spot a gap in the market, you're catching a glimpse of your potential income stream.

Next up, consider scalability. Your side hustle might begin small, but its ability to scale without an equal increase in active effort is where true passive income shines. Whether it's investing in dividend-yielding stocks or creating digital assets, pick paths that can grow. Will your product or service remain relevant as time ticks on? Is there room for it to expand, or will it be a flash in the pan?

Let's not forget about time investment. You've got 24 hours in a day, just like everyone else. Your passive income exploits should ideally afford you more freedom, not chain you to a desk. Vet your ideas against the time they require to set up and keep. opt for those that promise to become more passive as they mature.

We live in a digital renaissance, and online platforms have become a breeding ground for passive income prospects. Do you have a sizeable social media following? Monetize it through affiliate marketing or sponsored content. These opportunities didn't exist a couple of decades ago, and they're ripe for the picking if you've got the reach.

Financial resources are part of the equation, too. Gauge what you're willing to invest financially without jeopardizing your stability. Don't drain your savings on a whim – assess the risks and start with income ventures that align with your fiscal comfort zone. Remember, some passive income ideas require more capital upfront than others.

Risk tolerance is a personal matter. Are you the type who's ready to jump into the deep end or do you prefer to test the waters first? Your approach to potential income avenues should respect your risk comfort level. Less risky endeavors like creating an online course differ greatly from playing the real estate market. Both can be profitable, but their risk profiles vary dramatically.

Let's talk about diversification, shall we? Don't put all your eggs in one basket. Exploring different passive income ideas can help spread the risk and may even unlock new revenue sources you hadn't considered. Your blog could lead to an eBook, and that eBook could inspire an online course. Layering your income streams creates a more robust financial safety net.

Lastly, your mindset will either be your launchpad or your anchor. Cultivating a growth mindset primes you for success; it fuels your resilience and adaptability in the ever-evolving world of passive income. Embrace learning, remain flexible in your strategies, and treat setbacks as steppingstones. Your reaction to failure decides the height of your eventual success.

So, let's sum it up. Finding your passive income potential is about a candid self-assessment of your skills, interests, and resources. It's about keeping your eye on market demands, thinking big and scalable, calculating the investment of time and money, balancing risk, and diversifying your efforts. Bolster all of this with a steadfast mindset that's ever ready to learn and adjust.

Cultivate the ground for your passive income seeds with care. In the next sections, we'll dive deeper into specific strategies, tools, and pathways. But for now, understand that your potential for passive income is interwoven with the genuine value you can provide. So, take a thorough inventory of your unique combination of skills, assets, and passions. Your passive income potential isn't just about making money while you sleep; it's about creating a sustainable lifestyle that aligns with your entrepreneurial spirit and the value you bring to the world.

Remember, as you gear up to turn your potential into reality, every big journey begins with that first, intentional step. Start here, with a clear-eyed view of what you can offer, and the sky's the limit for where your passive income journey can take you.

Chapter 2

The Blueprint of Affiliate Marketing

Now that we've laid the groundwork for understanding the realm of passive income, let's delve into the rich tapestry that is affiliate marketing. Think of it as a puzzle. You've got your corner pieces with your basic understanding, but it's time to fill in the heart of the picture. The blueprint of affiliate marketing isn't just finding a few links and scattering them across the web; it's about creating a comprehensive ecosystem where content, products, and audience intersect. You'll learn to forge strong partnerships, select products that resonate with your niche, and set up a seamless system that promotes growth while you're knocking out other tasks or catching those Zs. Get ready to construct a structure that's robust and ready to stand the test of time, traffic, and trends. It's not just about making that first affiliate sale; we aim for a strategy that continues to pay dividends, building a robust foundation that sustains your financial goals with unwavering strength.

Setting Up Your Affiliate Marketing Ecosystem

As we turn the page from understanding the framework of passive income streams, it's time to build our foundation in the fertile grounds of affiliate marketing. The ecosystem of affiliate marketing isn't just a solitary tree but a complex forest, where each component interacts with others to grow and thrive. So, let's dig into the soil and plant the seeds that will blossom into your successful affiliate marketing venture.

First things first, you need a digital home base—a website or blog that reflects your brand and serves as the hub for your affiliate activities. Think of it as laying down the roots of your ecosystem. It's where you'll nurture your audience, showcase the products or services you promote, and ultimately where conversion magic happens. Ensure that your website is user-friendly, aesthetically pleasing, and, most importantly, perfected to encourage visitors to take action.

Now, don't just throw some random links up and call it a day. Your ecosystem must have symbiotic relationships. Remember, the products you choose to affiliate with should align with your brand's values and resonate with your audience. Picture your website as a garden—when you plant the right seeds (products) that match the soil's conditions (your audience's needs), they'll grow strongly and healthily.

Next up is the mighty email list. This isn't some outdated tactic—it's your secret weapon. Your email list enables you to send targeted traffic back to your website on demand. Think of it as the rain that nourishes your ecosystem. Cultivate it with care, provide value, and when the time is right, it will rain down conversions through strategic emails that highlight the affiliate offers that best serve your readers' needs.

An affiliate marketer's toolbox isn't complete without analytics. This is your feedback loop, allowing you to understand which parts of your ecosystem are thriving and which need some TLC. Use analytics to track which affiliate links are performing well and which ones are not. This data isn't just numbers; it's the compass that guides your strategy, helping you to adapt and optimize for better performance.

One does not simply walk into the realm of affiliate marketing alone. Partnerships with merchants and other affiliates can enrich your ecosystem considerably. Like pollinators in a garden, fostering good relationships with your partners can help spread the word about your website, bringing in a new audience and, in turn, more potential for earnings.

To maximize the fruits of your labor, you must use content as your sunlight. Without the warming, informative rays of high-quality, valuable content, your ecosystem's growth will be stunted. Whether it's reviews, how-to guides, or thought pieces, content done right attracts visitors, builds trust, and generates revenue.

On the note of trust, let's talk about reputation. Building a trusted brand in your affiliate marketing ecosystem isn't an overnight success; it's the result of consistent, authentic interactions with your audience. Much like a tree that takes time to grow, your reputation develops slowly with each blog post, newsletter, and social media interaction. Look after it, and it will support your ecosystem for years to come.

Social media platforms can act as extensions of your ecosystem, much like the branches of a tree. Each platform serves a different purpose and reaches different audiences. Use these platforms to engage with your community, share your content, and drive traffic back to your website. But remember, it's not enough just to be present; you have to be active and strategic to make those branches bear fruit.

Speaking of strategy, let's touch on diversification. Just as a healthy ecosystem has a variety of plants and animals, your affiliate marketing efforts should be varied. Relying on a single affiliate product or strategy is akin to planting a monoculture that's vulnerable to pests and disease. Instead, diversify your affiliate offers to protect your income from fluctuations and changes in the market.

The technical side of things is another important aspect of your ecosystem. This includes website speed, mobile optimization, and seamless check-out or lead capture processes. Your visitors are like wild animals in the forest; if they don't find what they need quickly and easily, they'll move on to greener pastures. So, it's crucial to ensure that your website and backend processes are smooth and efficient.

Don't underestimate the power of a calendar. A content and promotion schedule is like the seasons in your ecosystem. Plan out when you'll promote certain products and when to publish content related to them. This organized approach ensures that you're not just blindly scattering seeds but planting them at the most opportune time for them to sprout.

With the groundwork laid, it's important to also touch on legal considerations. Your affiliate marketing ecosystem must be compliant with laws and regulations. That means being transparent with your audience through disclaimers and adhering to the rules set out by affiliate programs and networks. These aren't just formalities; they're essential to maintaining a healthy, sustainable ecosystem.

Lastly, embrace the learning curve. The affiliate marketing landscape is ever-changing, which means there's always new knowledge to absorb and new techniques to apply. Stay curious and willing to innovate. As your ecosystem matures, you'll find that the lessons learned along the way are as valuable as the income earned.

By now, you've got a blueprint for setting up a robust affiliate marketing ecosystem that's ready to grow and prosper. Keep this ecosystem healthy with regular maintenance, effort, and passion, and it will reward you with a flourishing source of passive income. Don't rush the process; nurture it and let your perseverance and hard work pay off.

Remember, as we move forward through the following chapters, we'll delve deeper into the specifics of choosing partners, creating stellar content, and utilizing every tactic at your disposal to maximize your affiliate impact. For now, take pride in the vibrant ecosystem you're about to create. It's the foundation upon which your affiliate's success will be built.

Choosing the Right Partners and Products

Now, let's get down to brass tacks. You've got the framework of your affiliate marketing empire under construction, and it's looking good. But a structure is only as strong as its components, and in affiliate marketing, those components are your partnerships and the products you endorse. One wrong move here, and you could be hammering a nail in the coffin of your budding business.

First off, picking the right partners is critical. Think of it as dating – not every good looker is going to be a match for your soul. You need companies that resonate with your values and goals. Look for transparency and a solid track record. Scrutinize their affiliate programs like you're inspecting a diamond. The finer the cut, the brighter it sparkles. Payout structures, support systems, and their reputation, among other affiliates, are key sides to consider.

But it's not just the companies; it's also about the products. They must sing to your audience. Aligning product selections with what your crowd craves is crucial for conversion. If you're into tech, and your audience is a bunch of gadget gurus, don't try to peddle them pots and pans. You've got to be in sync with their desires like a playlist matches a road trip vibe.

Let's not forget, that wolves lurk in sheep's clothing. There are some companies out there looking to swindle both you and your audience. So, roll up your sleeves and do due diligence. Online forums, reviews, and testimonials can serve as your guide to detecting if there's something fishy going on.

Dip your toes in the water before diving in. Test out the products you want to promote. It's not just about making a quick buck; it's about building trust. You wouldn't recommend a restaurant without trying the cuisine first, right? It's the same principle. Your audience can spot a fake endorsement a mile away, and once trust is broken, it's harder than titanium to repair.

Contract terms can sometimes feel like you need a law degree to decipher them. Take your time and read them like it's the last book on earth. Look out for commission rates that change like the tides, and cookie durations that are as short-lived as a mayfly. These are the specifics that can make or break the profitability of your offers.

Remember, the internet is a constantly shifting landscape. What's hot today might just be tomorrow's cold leftovers. Stay on top of trends and predict where the wind is blowing. Your flexibility in switching products or partners when necessary is like having a good shock absorber—it makes for a much smoother ride.

Diversity isn't just a buzzword; it's your financial safety net. Don't put all your eggs in one partner's basket, no matter how golden it looks. The 21st-century business climate is unpredictable. If one stream dries up, you want to ensure that others can sustain you.

Customer feedback is like gold dust. Listen to it, cherish it, and let it guide your choices. If your audience raves about a product, you're onto a winner. If they're giving it the cold shoulder, it's time to reassess. Your audience's voice is the most valuable tool in your toolbox.

If the product or service requires too much of a hard sell, it might not be the right fit. You're looking for products that fit into your narrative as seamlessly as your favorite pair of jeans. If you must convince yourself of its value, you're going to strike out convincing others.

Networking with other affiliates can be your treasure trove of insight. They've been in the trenches and have seen what works and what digs a hole in your credibility. Connect, converse, and learn from them. They can give you the rundown on the industry do's and don'ts that could save you from a head-on collision.

Get analytical. Your website and social media analytics can tell you what's resonating with your peeps. This data isn't just numbers; it's the map to buried treasure. Products that are getting clicks, likes, and shares? That's where X marks the spot.

The fine print isn't there to be ignored. Grab those terms and conditions with both hands and work out every important detail. It's the small print that will tell you about any quotas or hidden fees that could ambush you down the line.

Quality over quantity, always. It's tempting to plaster your digital real estate with a cacophony of products but resist the urge. A select line of high-quality, relevant products will paint you as a trusted curator rather than a peddler at a flea market.

And finally, choose products that you're passionate about. It's easier to stay motivated and push through the tough times when you genuinely believe in what you're promoting. Your passion will light a fire in others, so let it shine!

In conclusion, selecting the right partners and products isn't just an item on your to-do list, it's the lifeblood of your affiliate marketing success. It demands your intuition and intellect in equal measure. Put the work in here, and you're setting the stage for a display of dazzling passive income fireworks. Make wise choices and watch as your side hustle grows into something others only dream about. You've got the power – now go ahead and use it.

Chapter 3

Content Creation for Affiliate Success

Imagine your content as the magnetic core of your affiliate marketing universe, it's the pull that snaps your readers' attention from the vastness of the Internet straight to your offerings—but only if it's stellar. Crafting content that resonates with your audience isn't just about slapping some text on a page; it's an art form that weaves together the threads of creativity, strategy, and an intimate understanding of your target audience. It's in these digital landscapes that you'll etch your mark, providing value-packed posts, reviews that build trust, and insightful videos that turn viewers into loyal followers—and buyers. The magic happens when you blend your unique voice with SEO-smart techniques, ensuring not just a fleeting spotlight but a lasting presence atop search engine results. You're in this to create ripples, not just to make a splash. Whether it's a blog post dissecting the pros and cons of the latest tech, or a tutorial series guiding newbies through their first online purchase—your content is the bridge between curiosity and conversion. So, let's dive deep into the world of content creation, where your words will become the catalyst for affiliate success and where each piece you craft is another step towards carving out your empire in the realms of passive income.

Crafting Compelling Content That Converts

Imagine you have two blog posts sitting in front of you. Both are aimed at promoting the same product. One is a bland regurgitation of product specifications, while the other narrates a story, weaving the product features into a tapestry of real-life benefits, vivid examples, and persuasive calls to action. Which one do you think will resonate with readers? Exactly. Crafting content that converts is an art form that blends strategy with storytelling, and it's crucial for driving successful affiliate marketing.

Churning out content is one thing, but creating material that captivates readers and motivates them to act—that's the golden ticket. It starts with understanding your audience. Who are they? What are their pain points? How can your content provide a solution? Offering solutions through your content in a way that feels organic and genuine is the first step in converting a reader into a customer.

Next, let's talk about headlines. They're the first thing your audience sees, and they make a big difference. The goal? Craft a headline so irresistible that bypassing it feels like a lost opportunity. Think curiosity-inducing, benefit-packed, and attention-grabbing. It's not just about being flashy; your headline must also align with the content that follows.

Now, the real meat of the matter—your content. It should be rich in value, packed with insights, and devoid of fluff. Each word should earn its place on the page. This means doing your homework, getting to know the product or service inside out, and finding unique angles to present it to your readers. The content should quench the reader's thirst for knowledge and leave them hungry for the solution you're providing.

Everyone has a story, and your content should too. Storytelling isn't just for fiction; it's a powerful tool in marketing. Infusing narrative elements makes your content memorable and relatable. When someone sees themselves in your writing, you've created a connection. And connections lead to conversions.

Varying your content types also keeps your audience engaged. Don't just write blog posts. Create infographics, videos, or podcasts. Play with lists, how-tos, and case studies. Experimenting with different formats can help you find what resonates best with your audience and what most effectively showcases affiliate products.

Let's not forget the importance of SEO—though that's a topic we'll delve into more deeply in another section. For now, understand that integrating relevant keywords into your content organically is essential. It makes your content discoverable, which is the precursor to it being consumable and, ultimately, convertible.

The art of persuasion is subtle. Your content should educate and engage, but also gently guide the reader towards a course of action. This could be subscribing to a newsletter, sharing the post, or purchasing a product. Calls to action (CTAs) should be clear and compelling, but not overbearing. A well-placed CTA in the flow of content can make all the difference between contemplation and conversion.

Offering evidence is one way to boost credibility. Reviews, testimonials, comparisons, and case studies are influential because they offer social proof. Sharing success stories or endorsements from others builds trust, and trust is a cornerstone of effective content.

Understanding the psychology of persuasion is a weapon in your arsenal. Concepts such as scarcity, authority, and commitment can all be woven into your content strategy. Used ethically, these triggers can lead to higher conversion rates because they speak to the subconscious drivers of decision-making.

Of course, creating compelling content is not a set-it-and-forget-it deal. You've got to monitor, analyze, and iterate. Use the data at your disposal, from click-through rates to time on page, to understand what's working and what's not. Then, refine your approach. Continuous improvement is key to staying relevant and keeping your content conversion friendly.

Consistency in publishing content is another important piece of the puzzle. It's not just about quantity but creating a regular rhythm of quality content that trains your readers to look forward to your next post, infographic, or video. Building this kind of anticipation is essential for keeping and growing a dedicated audience.

However, let's also acknowledge that creating content doesn't necessarily equate to reinventing the wheel every time. Repurposing successful content into other formats or updating existing material can also drive conversions. It's about maximizing the reach and lifespan of your best work.

Lastly, let's circle back to the importance of connection. Authenticity trumps forced sales pitches any day. Be genuine, transparent, and human in your writing. People can sense when content is disingenuous, and nothing puts up barriers faster than insincerity. Your voice should be a trustworthy one in the conversation, guiding them to make informed decisions.

Composing content that converts is the linchpin of any affiliate marketing strategy. It's the wellspring where passive income begins to bubble up. Remember, content that converts doesn't strong-arm. It inspires, educates, and enlightens. When done right, it doesn't feel like a pitch—it feels like a conversation. A conversation that leads not only to a sale but to the start of a relationship with your reader that can blossom into loyalty and advocacy. That's the sweet spot where content becomes not just compelling, but truly transformative in building your passive income empire.

Leveraging SEO for Long-Term Traffic

Imagine the internet as an ever-expanding metropolis, with your content as a storefront. In this vast cityscape, to be seen by potential customers, you need your sign to be loud, clear, and visible to anyone passing by. That's where SEO comes into the picture. SEO, or Search Engine Optimization, is the art and science of making your online content more attractive to search engines like Google. It's a cornerstone of your content creation, critical for the longevity of your traffic, and, by extension, your passive income potential.

Diving into SEO begins with understanding keywords. These are the bread and butter of SEO strategies. As an entrepreneur or a blogger, you want to think like your audience. They're out there, typing questions and phrases into search bars, looking for the content you're creating. But if your content doesn't include the words they are searching for, they'll never find you. It's vital to conduct thorough keyword research, discover exactly what your target audience is searching for, and seamlessly integrate these terms into your content in a way that feels natural and valuable.

Content is king, sure, but only if it's structured properly. Search engines love content that's not only relevant but also easy to understand. This means organizing your material with the use of headers, bullet points, and paragraphs that enhance readability. But here's the twist: while you must appeal to the algorithms, don't forget that humans are your primary readers. Write for them first—clear, engaging, and informative content always wins the race.

Now, let's talk about consistency. Search engines adore websites that are routinely updated with fresh content. If you're constantly producing and publishing new material, search engines view your site as an active and valuable source of information. This leads to improved rankings, which is the equivalent of moving your online storefront to a main street with heavy foot traffic. More visibility means more potential customers and better chances for that affiliate marketing income to grow.

Backlinks are another crucial ingredient in the SEO stew. They're essentially votes of confidence from other reputable websites. Picture them like endorsements from locals in our metaphorical city. The more you get, the more search engines trust your site as a credible source. Gaining backlinks requires crafting share-worthy content and networking with other webmasters, but the effort is worth it for the traffic boost it can bring.

Technical SEO also can't be ignored. It's like the plumbing and electrical work in your store. If those aren't up to code, it doesn't matter how good your products are—customers will have a hard time accessing them. This means optimizing your site's speed, mobile-friendliness, and indexability. Search engines prefer sites that load quickly, look good on all devices, and have a clear structure that their bots can easily navigate.

User experience is, at the end of the day, the pinnacle. You can't just bring someone to your doorstep; you've got to ensure they enjoy their stay. Sites that provide a superior user experience (like intuitive navigation and fast load times) signal to search engines that you're providing value to visitors. This can lead to better search rankings and, again, more traffic to monetize.

Local SEO is a powerful tool if you're targeting a specific geography. This entails optimizing your content for location-based searches. It works wonders for brick-and-mortar businesses, but don't dismiss it for your online ventures. You can engage with local audiences who might be looking for solutions nearby, even if digitally. This targeted approach can be particularly effective for specialized niches that appeal to certain locales.

The use of rich snippets and structured data is an advanced technique but pays ample dividends. By marking up your content and providing explicit clues about its meaning, you can help search engines present your content in a more attractive and informative way in search results. This includes things like ratings, prices, or author information. It's like having an eye-catching sign with the best deals written in bold for everyone to see; it draws the eye and the click.

Long-form content gets much love from search engines due to the depth and value it tends to provide. This doesn't mean every piece should be a novella, but it does mean investing time in comprehensive guides and in-depth explorations of topics related to your niche. These kinds of pieces can become evergreen content that consistently draws traffic, shows your authority, and builds trust with your audience.

But where many get caught up is the fear of change, as search engine algorithms are constantly evolving. What works today might not work tomorrow. However, it's crucial to stay informed and adapt your strategies. Think of flexibility and a willingness to learn as part of your business's infrastructure. Continual learning keeps you ahead of the curve, turns potential obstacles into steppingstones, and ensures that your traffic continues to flow.

Measuring and analyzing your SEO efforts is how you fine-tune your engine. Use tools like Google Analytics to keep a close eye on which pages are pulling their weight and which might need a revamp. Like reviewing your financial statements, this data-driven approach helps you make decisions based on what affects your bottom line: clicks and conversions.

Remember, while SEO may seem technical, at its heart, it boils down to providing the best answer to someone's question at exactly the right time. It's about being present, providing value, and building authority in your space. When you successfully manage that, search engines take notice, and traffic starts to become less of a quick win and more of a sustainable resource.

In a sense, effective SEO is about building a legacy—each piece of content contributes to a compendium of knowledge that defines your brand and draws an audience. Your passive income is directly fed by the ebb and flow of this traffic, and by using SEO effectively, you're setting up streams that flow for the long haul.

So, it's time to take control and make SEO a priority in your content creation efforts, nurturing it to ensure that traffic never trickles to a stop. With solid SEO, you're not just a flash in the pan of internet content; you're building a beacon that continually guides potential customers to your door, all hours of the day—a true foundation for sustainable passive income.

Chapter 4

Maximizing Your Online Presence

Diving headfirst into Chapter 4, it's high time we supercharged that digital footprint of yours, transforming it into a magnet for opportunity and profit. You've nailed down crafting content that sizzles with value, and now, it's about amplifying its reach to the max. Imagine your online presence as a beacon, one that shines the spotlight on your brand, luring in wanderers from the far corners of the internet. We will optimize every tweet, every post, and every share to set the virtual stage for your affiliate triumphs. This isn't just about being visible—it's about being unforgettable. And don't think it's all down to luck; with the right blogging tactics and a savvy approach to social media, tools that we'll be unraveling in this chapter, you'll watch your influence skyrocket, engagement soar, and yes, those passive income streams you've dreamt of will start to pour in. So, let's grab the digital world by the horns and show it what you're made of!

Blogging Strategies for Affiliate Marketers

As an affiliate marketer delving into the realm of blogging, it's essential to craft a strategy that not only draws readers into your world but also encourages them to make purchases through your affiliate links. Your blog isn't just a collection of articles; it's a bustling marketplace, a cozy coffee shop where conversations turn into conversions. So, let's dive into the strategies that will help transform your blog into a powerhouse of affiliate success.

Firstly, understanding the audience you're writing for is the bedrock of affiliate marketing. It's fruitless to promote products to an audience with no interest in them. You've got to get up close and personal – figure out their dreams, their problems, and how the products you promote can swoop in as their knight in shining armor. Craft content with purpose and precision, tailor it like a custom suit, each thread woven with the desires and needs of your audience in mind.

Next up, harness the power of storytelling. You're not just selling a product, you're narrating a tale, where the product plays the hero, solving problems and bestowing benefits. Weave stories that make your readers picture themselves using the products; let their imaginations run wild until they can't help but desire that experience for themselves. Your blog posts should tell a story that leads seamlessly into the introduction of your affiliate products.

Keep your ear to the ground and your content fresh. Trends come and go, and your blog needs to keep pace. Stay updated on the latest in your niche and be quick to adjust your content calendar accordingly. When you're one of the first to break the news or offer guidance on fresh trends, you position your blog as a leading authority — and search engines love that, so expect a little SEO love too.

Speaking of SEO, remember it's a critical player in this game. Use relevant keywords that don't just sprinkle but pour into the crevices of the search engine algorithms. But don't stuff 'em like a Thanksgiving turkey; keep it organic, natural, and flowing. Your aim is to rank high in search results and become the go-to resource when someone is seeking information on the products in your niche.

Blend your affiliate promotions with your content – subtly. Like a master chef, your job is to blend ingredients so no one flavor overpowers the other. Your affiliate links should feel like a natural part of your content, not an afterthought. Educate first, sell second. By providing immense value before pushing a product, you create a relationship rooted in trust.

Utilize compelling CTAs (calls-to-action). Each post should guide your reader on what to do next. Whether it's to "Learn More", "Buy Now", or "Get a Discount", your CTAs should be clear and tantalizing, drawing the reader in. And don't just slap them at the end; incorporate them strategically throughout your content.

Don't be afraid to experiment with different content types. Your blog could include in-depth guides, reviews, comparisons, listicles, and even personal stories related to the products you're promoting. Different audiences prefer different types of content, so mixing it up can widen your reach and appeal.

Consistency is critical. Establish a posting schedule and stick to it like glue. Your readers should know when to expect new content from you – it is all part of building a loyal following. Plus, regular updates boost SEO and keep your blog in the good grace of search engines.

Engage with your readers in the comments. The conversation shouldn't end at your conclusion. Interact, answer questions, and give more advice – it humanizes your brand and shows you're not just a faceless marketer. Plus, a lively comments section can enhance SEO and keep readers on your page longer, which signals to search engines that your content is valuable.

Track your results and tweak them accordingly. Which articles are getting the most traffic? Which affiliate links are getting the most clicks? Use tools to analyze this data and understand what's working and what isn't. Be ready to pivot; adaptability is your friend in the fast-paced world of blogging and affiliate marketing.

Network with other bloggers in your niche. This isn't a solitary journey; it's a community effort. Guest posts, collaborations, and shout-outs can introduce you to new audiences and build authority. Plus, you'll gain invaluable insights and potentially beneficial partnerships.

Don't ignore the importance of design and usability. Your blog should be easy on the eyes and even easier to navigate. A clunky, antiquated website will drive readers away faster than you can say 'bounce rate'. Ensure your loading times are quick, your layout is clean, and your affiliate links work flawlessly.

Lastly, never stop learning and evolving. The affiliate marketing landscape is a shifting terrain; you've got to be an intrepid explorer, always ready for uncharted territories. Stay updated on best practices, experiment with new techniques, and refine your strategy with each new piece of insight.

When you commit to these strategies, your blog becomes a finely tuned machine, humming with the energy of potential sales. And remember, it's not just about the numbers, but the genuine value you provide. Focus on creating content that informs, entertains, and solves problems, and affiliate success will follow. Your blog is the gateway to your audience's heart and mind. Nurture it, cherish it, and watch as it transforms into a cornerstone of your passive income stream.

Forge ahead with confidence, creativity, and determination. You don't just want your slice of the pie; you're baking the whole dessert. Now, let's transition seamlessly to our next topic and discover how to utilize social media platforms effectively, further expanding your online empire and accelerating your journey toward financial freedom.

Utilizing Social Media Platforms Effectively

The digital landscape is vast, and social media is arguably its most vibrant neighborhood. For the entrepreneurial spirits harnessing the power of affiliate marketing, being adept with these platforms can be the difference between a fledgling side hustle and a flourishing income stream.

Let's dive into tactics to turn likes, shares, and follows into a robust support system for your passive income goals. First and foremost, it is critical to understand each platform's unique language and demographic. Facebook's community, for instance, values personal storytelling and connection, while Instagram lovers crave aesthetically pleasing visuals and concise messaging. Meanwhile, LinkedIn's professional network is the perfect stage for thought leadership and expert advice.

The magic begins with consistency. Establishing a regular posting schedule keeps your audience engaged and anticipation high. This doesn't mean flooding feeds with content but finding that sweet spot where your presence is welcome, not overwhelming. Through consistency, you create touchpoints that foster relationships and trust, paving the way for affiliate product recommendations.

Content is king in the social media realm, but context is its queen. Tailoring your posts to suit the platform will use native behavior. For instance, a tweet is fleeting and requires snappy, impactful words, while a YouTube video gives room to delve deep into product reviews or tutorials. By considering these contexts, you can craft messages that resonate and drive action.

Interactivity is your golden ticket. Social media thrives on two-way conversations. Run polls, ask for opinions, and engage directly with comments. This not only boosts your algorithmic appeal but also signals that you value your followers' voices. It turns passive scrollers into active participants in your digital ecosystem.

Pair your organic efforts with strategic paid campaigns. Advertising on social platforms can amplify your reach, especially when targeting is precise. Drill down to interests, behaviors, and demographics that mirror your ideal customer. Craft compelling ads that feel as natural as organic content to seamlessly weave your affiliate links into your audience's social experience.

Analytics should be your compass guiding you through the social media wilderness. Track engagement rates, click-throughs, and conversion metrics to refine your approach. A post that resonates will have a clear signature in its numbers. Use this data to home in on what works and cut loose strategies that don't deliver.

Next up, tap into the power of storytelling. You're not just selling a product; you're tying it into a narrative that aligns with your audience's values and lifestyle. Visuals, anecdotes, and testimonials can all be part of this narrative, making your affiliate products not just a commodity but a piece of a larger story your followers want to be a part of.

Collaborations can be your ace in the hole. Partner with influencers and other brands that align with your affiliate offerings to tap into new audiences. These relationships can yield content that is mutually beneficial, sharing credibility, and exposure.

Influencer marketing isn't just for the heavy hitters. Micro-influencers, with their niche followings, can provide a high level of engagement and trust. Connect with them to create a more targeted, authentic approach to promoting your affiliate products.

Don't underestimate the power of a hashtag. They're not just trendy; they're tools that slice through the noise, connecting your content with interested communities. Research and use relevant hashtags to get your posts discovered by those looking for exactly what you're offering.

User-generated content (UGC) is a treasure trove that's often overlooked. Encourage your audience to share their experiences with your affiliate products. Not only does this provide social proof, but it also generates content for you to share, displaying real-life validation of the value you're promoting.

Your profile is your digital storefront, so perfect it. Ensure that links to your blog or website are prominent, bios are updated, and contact information is clear. The easier it is for people to find and follow through to your affiliate links, the smoother the transition from browser to buyer.

Timing can be as important as content. Leverage peaks when your audience is most active to boost visibility. While it's essential to be mindful of global time zones if your audience is international, don't overlook the value of timely reactions to current events and trends to keep your content fresh and relevant.

Finally, safeguarding your reputation should underscore every action. Transparency about affiliate links and preserving the integrity of your recommendations will solidify the trust and respect of your audience. Always show partnership and keep the quality of your endorsements to ensure long-term success.

To wrap up, navigating social media as a force for your passive income is both an art and a science. Blend creativity with strategic thinking and infuse your personality across platforms to cultivate genuine connections. Treat your social presence not as a megaphone but as an extension of your value proposition, where every interaction could open the door to a new supporter of your passive income journey. So, harness the full spectrum of social media to empower and energize your entrepreneurial endeavors—it's a realm ripe with opportunity for those ready to engage it with heart and savvy.

Chapter 5

Building and Engaging Your Audience

Coming out of the trenches of content creation and seamless integration on social media, it's high time to dive headlong into the crux of any successful online endeavor - your audience. Feel the pulse of your niche; it's about getting into the groove of their needs, wants, and midnight musings. To ignite that spark and foster a blazing fire, you've got to connect, engage, and wow your audience with every click they make. Think of it like hosting the ultimate soiree; be that person everyone's drawn to, chatting with, sharing moments with — that's when you know you've got 'em. It's more than just numbers; it's about real people, with real dreams, all looking for that gem you're poised to offer. So, let's get personal, let's get real, and let's turn those casual visitors into loyal fans, customers, and heck, even brand ambassadors. It's not just about reaching out; it's about reaching deep. Because at the end of the day, a vibrant, engaged community is the powerhouse that drives passive income into a steady, thrumming reality.

Email Marketing Mastery

As an entrepreneur, blogger, or side hustle superstar, you're already juggling many balls in the air. Let's zero in on one that can remarkably amplify your success: email marketing. This powerhouse tool, when wielded with skill, can become a critical part of your strategy to cultivate sustainable passive income streams. It's intimate, direct, and, most importantly, incredibly effective.

First, let's tackle the 'why' behind email marketing. In the digital age, emails are personal envelopes of opportunity landing directly in someone's virtual mailbox. Unlike the fleeting nature of social media posts or the broad net of blog readership, emails allow you to speak one-on-one with your audience. And guess what? People still read emails. A well-crafted email doesn't just get opened; it gets read, contemplated, and can move subscribers to action.

Creating an email list is like striking gold in the marketing world. Your list is a catalog of individuals who have shown interest in your offerings—what you say and what you sell. It's your job to nurture that list. Think of it as a garden; with attentive care, your subscriber list can bloom, spreading its influence everywhere. Always prioritize quality over quantity; a smaller, engaged audience is far more valuable than a vast, indifferent one.

When crafting your emails, remember the power of personalization. Personalized emails aren't just a name at the top; they cater content to the individual's preferences and behaviors. Segmentation is your friend here. By grouping your subscribers based on their interests or past interactions with your brand, you can tailor your messages to resonate more deeply. Remember, if an email feels bespoke (without using the term), it becomes more meaningful to the recipient.

Now, about those emails themselves: they're not just digital letters; they're strategic tools crafted to add value and increase engagement. Each email should give more than it takes. Share insights, tips, or inspirational stories. Make your subscribers feel like they're gaining something just by opening your message. This is not only good manners—it's smart business.

We can't talk about emails without discussing the infamous call-to-action (CTA). This isn't just a button or a line of text—it's the hinge on which the door to opportunity swings. Your CTA should be clear, compelling, and drive to a single action you want the reader to take. Whether it's to check out your latest blog post, learn more about a product, or take advantage of a special offer, your CTA should be impossible to ignore. Use action words and create a sense of urgency.

Let's not forget the design aspect. In our modern visual world, a plain text email can be just as effective as a beautifully designed HTML template—it all depends on your audience and the message you want to send. However, never let design overpower content. The aesthetic should support your message, not distract from it. And always ensure your emails are mobile-friendly; with most people tackling their inboxes on the go, readability is key.

Remember, email marketing is a game of consistency. If you drop in and out of your subscribers' inboxes erratically, you're missing out on the chance to build a relationship. Whether it's a weekly newsletter or a monthly update, find a rhythm that works for you and stick to it. Consistency builds trust, and trust leads to loyalty.

It's also essential to analyze your results regularly. Email marketing platforms come with a treasure trove of analytics. Open rates, click-through rates, and conversions are more than just metrics; they're insights into what's working and what's not. Use this data to refine your strategies, test different approaches, and continually improve your email game.

But beware of the pitfalls. With great power comes great responsibility. Never spam your audience or buy lists. It's unethical, and frankly, it'll tarnish your brand's reputation. Embrace the slow and steady growth of a list built on authentic connections and real interest in what you're putting into the world.

A/B testing is another trick of the trade. Tweaking subject lines or the placement of a CTA button might seem negligible, but these slight changes can have outsize impacts on the effectiveness of your campaigns. Test, tweak, and test again. It's a never-ending cycle, but one that sharpens the effectiveness of your emails over time.

For those subscribers who've drifted, a re-engagement campaign can work wonders. Remind them why they loved you in the first place with a heartfelt 'We Miss You' and perhaps an exclusive offer. Not everyone will come back, but those who do often return more engaged than before.

Compliance is critical. Make sure you stay up to date with regulations like the CAN-SPAM Act and GDPR for your European subscribers. Being complaint isn't just about avoiding fines—it's about respecting your subscribers and creating a safe space for communication.

And lastly, remember that email marketing is a relationship-building tool. Beyond sales, beyond metrics—it's about forging connections. Author your emails like you're writing to a friend, with warmth and genuine interest in their well-being. Because in the end, the relationships you cultivate will be the foundation upon which your passive income streams thrive.

I hope this dive into email marketing mastery inspires you to use this fantastic tool's full potential. As you move through the journey of growing your online presence and automation, keep circling back to your emails—a personal touch in an increasingly impersonal digital landscape. Happy mailing!

Community Building and Customer Retention moves us beyond the mechanics of setting up platforms and creating content. It's about nurturing the individuals who click, comment, and, most importantly, convert. These are the folks who'll vouch for your brand, purchase through your affiliate links time and again, and become the foundation of your passive income empire.

Let's face it; snagging a new customer is thrilling. But that thrill pales in comparison to the sustained joy of seeing the same names pop up in your sales notifications. That's where the real growth potential lies. Recurring customers can generate more revenue over time than multiple one-offs ever could. But how do you transform a first-time buyer into a loyal follower?

It begins with a mindset shift. See your audience not just as customers but as a community. A community is dynamic, engaging, and connected. It's about shared values and common goals. And in the affiliate marketing realm, it means fostering a space where your content resonates so deeply that people can't wait to share it and come back for more.

Creating that bond takes authenticity and transparency. When you share your journey, including your successes and hiccups, you're not just a vendor; you're a fellow traveler on the path to success. Your recommendations carry weight because they're based on real experiences, not just empty pitches. It's about trust, and trust is the bedrock of any lasting relationship.

Engagement is not a one-way street. When someone takes the time to comment on your blog or social media posts, that's an opportunity. Engage with them. Answer their questions, thank them for their insights, and provide value wherever you can. Acknowledgment can go a long way; it confirms they're not just shouting into the void and that there's a real person on the other side who cares.

Diversifying your content to keep it fresh and relevant is crucial. Yes, your core message and niche won't wildly fluctuate, but the way you deliver it must evolve. Sometimes it's a deep-dive blog post, other times it's a quick yet informative video. Change it up to cater to different segments within your community who consume content in many ways.

Next up, custom experiences. What we're talking about here is personalization. The more you can tailor the user experience to individual preferences and behaviors, the more valued and understood your community members will feel. This can be as simple as segmenting your email list to ensure that subscribers only receive content that's relevant to them.

Without a doubt, exclusive content or deals for your community members can reinforce their decision to stay connected with you. Access to webinars, eBooks, or discount codes for the products you promote can make community members feel like VIPs and increase their investment in your brand.

Social proof is powerful. When your community members rave about you or the products you recommend, others listen. Featuring success stories or testimonials on your platforms not only confirms your work but also motivates others to join the community and engage at a deeper level.

Building a community also means offering support. Whether it's addressing concerns about a product you promote or helping someone navigate their purchase, support shows that you're invested in their satisfaction and success beyond the sale.

Remember, retention is a byproduct of continuous effort. Check in with your community regularly, not just with promotions, but with surveys or informal chats about their needs and interests. Their feedback is gold, guiding your content strategy and ensuring that your efforts align with their evolving desires.

Let's not overlook collaboration. Sometimes, the best way to strengthen your community is by introducing them to other content creators or brands with complementary visions. This can expand the breadth of value you provide and signal to your community that you're plugged into the broader landscape of their interests.

A commitment to consistency in your messaging and your presence builds a rhythm that your community can depend on. Whether it's your email newsletter dropping out on Tuesdays or a weekly roundup of industry news, make sure your community knows when and where they can expect to connect with you and your content.

To cap it off, you've got to keep the circle virtuous. Reward your loyal followers with acknowledgment and incentivization. A referral program that helps both your existing community and new members can stimulate a growth loop, driven by the very people who already love what you do.

In summary, community building and customer retention are not just about keeping your sales steady. They're about creating an ecosystem where people feel valued, involved, and excited to be a part of what you're building. As an entrepreneur, blogger, or side hustler looking to craft sustainable passive income streams, these relationships are priceless. They're the bridge between a one-time transaction and a lifetime of mutual benefit and shared success. Invest in your community and watch as it becomes the backbone of your passive income journey.

Chapter 6

Automation and Scaling

So, you've laid the groundwork for your passive income stream, and you're catching the drift of how this all plays out. That's fantastic! Now, let's shift gears to something that's going to blow your mind: Automation and Scaling. Imagine having your passive income machine not just ticking over but hurtling forward, with you in the driver's seat, your foot relaxed on the pedal. That's what we're gearing towards. In this vitally important chapter, we introduce tools that are practically your clones; they'll work tirelessly, monitoring, adjusting, and optimizing your affiliate marketing campaigns while you sip your coffee. We're talking digital alchemy that turns time into money without you lifting a finger. And just when you think you've hit the ceiling, we'll show you how to burst through it with scaling strategies that multiply your success. It's about clever investment of resources, seizing opportunities, and supercharging your revenue—the smart way. Remember, scaling is an art, and with automation as your brush, the canvas is all yours.

Tools for Automating Your Affiliate Business

Imagine if you could flip a switch and have your affiliate business run like a well-oiled machine, freeing up your time to focus on creative growth or simply enjoy the thrills of entrepreneurial freedom. Well, the good news is you don't have to imagine. Automation tools have made this a tangible reality. Harnessing the power of technology isn't just a luxury anymore; it's a necessity for scaling your operations and maintaining a competitive edge without burning out.

Starting with affiliate management software, the beauty of these systems rests in their ability to streamline your affiliate partnerships. They provide a centralized platform for tracking clicks, managing payouts, and checking the performance of your affiliate links. **ShareASale, Clickbank, Commission Junction, and Digistore24.com** are just a couple of standouts in this space. They'll keep your finances in check and let you visualize which partnerships are bringing in the bacon, so you can make data-driven decisions on where to focus your efforts.

Email marketing automation can't be overlooked when you're building an affiliate empire. With tools like **Convert Kit** or **Mailchimp**, you can nurture leads and send your subscribers personalized content at scale. These services offer pre-built templates and workflows that make it easy to send out targeted campaigns, follow-ups, and newsletters to keep your audience engaged and clicking through your affiliate links.

Social media is a behemoth in the affiliate marketing landscape, and it's essential to stay active and responsive across your accounts. Yet, keeping it up can be a full-time job. That's where scheduling tools such as Buffer or Hootsuite come in handy. Set up a content calendar, schedule posts in bulk, and manage your social media interactions in one dashboard. This way, your presence stays consistent while the actual time you spend on social media plummets.

Content is king, but creation can be quite time-consuming. Thankfully, WordPress plugins like the **AffiliateWP** allow for smooth integration of affiliate links into your content, and AI-powered writing assistants can provide you with a solid starting point to craft your posts. Combine these tools with SEO software such as **SEMrush** or **Arefs** to generate organic search traffic to your site, thereby creating a seamless funnel of eyes to your affiliate offers.

Landing pages are critical to conversions, and tools like **Lead pages** or **Click Funnels** streamline the process of creating high-converting pages. They offer drag-and-drop builders and A/B testing capabilities, helping you hone the perfect page without needing a degree in web design or the budget to hire a developer.

For you to truly get a handle on your affiliate business's analytics, it's important to make friends with tools like Google Analytics or Clicky. They provide insightful data about who's visiting your site, what they're looking at, and how they interact with your content. Use this intel to tweak your strategy on the fly, ensuring your offerings align perfectly with what your audience desires.

Regarding productivity, project management tools such as Asana or Trello are indispensable. They can help you organize tasks, manage projects, and collaborate with any team members or freelancers you work with. Structure your affiliate marketing tasks into different projects, set deadlines, and monitor progress to keep everything moving forward.

Customer Relationship Management (CRM) software is also an essential part for scaling your affiliate business. Systems like Salesforce and HubSpot CRM allow you to keep detailed records of customer interactions, purchase history, and preferences. This enables personalized communication at scale, fostering a sense of trust and connection with your audience.

But what about those annoying repetitive tasks? Enter the magic of tools like **Zapier** or **Integromat**. They allow you to connect different apps and automate workflows. For example, you could set up a 'Zap' that automatically adds new email subscribers to a Google Sheets document or lets you know via Slack if there's a spike in affiliate sales.

Okay, so you've got many potential customers on your site – now what? It's time for chatbots and AI support tools to shine. They can oversee initial customer inquiries, provide immediate responses, and even guide users toward your affiliate products, all without your direct involvement.

Every savvy entrepreneur knows that an essential part of managing a successful affiliate business is keeping track of the finances. QuickBooks or FreshBooks can simplify this often-grueling task with their accounting and invoicing capabilities. They help track expenses and income, send automated reminders for invoices, and even manage payroll if you have a growing team.

Lastly, let's not forget about security and backup solutions. Just imagine the horror of losing all your carefully curated content and customer data due to a website crash. To prevent such disasters, rely on tools like **Updraft Plus** for WordPress to back up your data, or **Sucuri** for comprehensive website security that guards against malware and breaches.

Automating your affiliate business is like setting up a team of tireless digital workers, each excelling in their specific task, working around the clock. Using these tools collectively shapes a formidable backend that keeps you at the forefront of the affiliate marketing game. You'll be able to focus more on big-picture strategies and less on the daily grind. This is how you create a business that runs and thrives, even when you step away from the desk.

Nurturing a passive income source until it blossoms into a large stream requires some hard work at first, yes. But with the right suite of tools, this journey can be smarter, not harder. Now more than ever, it's about working strategically. Use technology to take on the brunt of the legwork, and let your human touch be reserved for the creativity and relationship-building that machines can't replicate. That's how you'll cultivate a flourishing affiliate business that stands the test of time and technology.

Strategies for Scaling Up Your Income - as we turn the page on automation and look towards multiplying our fiscal potential, it's important to pivot our discussion to strategic scaling. Whether you're a budding entrepreneur, a seasoned blogger, or someone weaving a side hustle into the tapestry of their daily life, scaling up requires more than just hard work—it requires smart work. And that's precisely what we're diving into.

Now that you've grasped automating your affiliate business, it's time to look at strategies that can exponentially increase your income. The concept is straightforward: use your current successes and expand upon them. Let's explore methods that have helped countless others transform their income from a steady stream into a surging river.

Firstly, understand the importance of reinvestment. Profits are not simply there for personal consumption; they fuel your business's engine. Returning funds to your venture can mean anything from upgrading your technology to investing in targeted advertising or enhancing your content quality. Each dollar reinvested wisely is a step towards amplified earnings.

Another key strategy is to diversify your income streams. Don't put all your eggs in one basket, as the saying goes. Look for complementary affiliate products or services to promote. This not only spreads risk but also opens new revenue channels. You'll likely discover that your audience has diverse interests—catering to these can be lucrative.

Collaboration is also a potent tool for scaling up. Networking with others in your field can lead to joint ventures, where you can combine your resources for greater impact. It's about synergy—finding ways to enhance each other's strengths while compensating for weaknesses.

Scaling requires measurement. You can't manage what you can't measure. Analyzing your traffic, sales, and conversion rates gives you valuable insights into what works and what doesn't. Only by understanding this data can you tweak your approach to perfect revenue.

Upselling and cross-selling to your existing customer base is another valuable strategy. If someone has already bought through your affiliate link once, they are more likely to do so again. Offer them added value through related products or services to increase the lifetime value of each customer.

Don't overlook the power of pricing strategies. Sometimes, adjusting the price points of the products you're promoting, if within your control, or offering bundles can significantly impact your commissions. Testing and adjustment are crucial here—find the sweet spot that maximizes sales while keeping value to the customer clear.

Going global can also unlock new income potential. The internet has a worldwide reach, and so should your affiliate marketing efforts. Localizing content and participating in affiliate programs with a global footprint can attract customers from various regions and time zones.

Investing in your education continually is another strategy that pays dividends. The online marketing landscape is ever-changing. Today's winning strategy could be tomorrow's outdated tactic. Keep up with industry trends, tools, and best practices through courses, webinars, and books.

Optimizing your sales funnel can lead to higher conversion rates. A well-designed, user-friendly funnel will guide visitors smoothly from discovery to buying. Each step should be as frictionless as possible to minimize drop-off rates and boost sales.

Moreover, improving your offer can increase your income significantly. Sometimes an extra bonus or a guarantee can make your affiliate offer stand out. Whether it's an eBook, a complimentary consultation, or a unique tool, try to offer something that adds undeniable value.

Consider building a team when the workload gets too heavy. Outsourcing tasks to freelancers or hiring employees allows you to focus on strategy and growth. Delegation is not an admission of defeat; it's a sign of a maturing business.

And let's not forget innovation. Be open to experimenting with innovative ideas. Whether it's launch jacking—a strategy where you promote new products right at their launch to ride the wave of initial buzz—or entering a new market niche, innovation keeps things fresh and your income upward.

Lastly, always prioritize customer satisfaction. Satisfied customers become repeat buyers and advocates for your brand. Word-of-mouth referrals can significantly increase your affiliate sales without any added marketing expenses.

In conclusion, scaling your income in the affiliate marketing space is not just about working harder but working smarter. It involves investment, diversification, education, optimization, and continual innovation. With these strategies in hand, you are well poised to elevate your passive income streams to new heights, transforming not just your bank account but your life's trajectory. Remember, your income is a direct reflection of the value you offer. Continuously seek ways to deliver more, and your income will scale up in concert.

Chapter 7

Overcoming Challenges and Setbacks

Look, every entrepreneur's journey is riddled with potholes and unexpected detours. In this high-stakes game of chess called business, sometimes it feels like you're a knight surrounded by pawns, with every move bringing you one step closer to checkmate by circumstances beyond your control. But here's the thing: resilience is born from adversity. You might hit a profit plateau, meet a market shift, or face an algorithm update that turns your traffic to a trickle. That's just the reality. Yet, what sets apart the go-getters from the no-getters isn't just the hustle—it's the ability to adapt, stand back up, dust off, and strategize anew. In Chapter 7, we're diving deep into the world of comeback stories. You'll learn how to spot those challenges from a mile away, grab them by the horns, and wrestle them into opportunities that leave you stronger than before. Whether it's pivoting your approach, tweaking your content, or rethinking your audience engagement, it all comes down to mindset. So, let's turn that setback into a setup for your greatest comeback ever, and remember, every challenge is just a hidden opportunity waiting to be unleashed.

Navigating the Common Pitfalls At some point along your passive income journey, you're going to face obstacles that have the potential to derail your progress. It's not a matter of if they will occur, but when. The pitfalls are numerous, but they don't have to spell doom for your endeavors. In fact, many of your peers have stumbled into – and climbed out of – similar trenches. Let's discuss strategies for maintaining your footing, even when the path gets slippery.

Firstly, it's essential to let go of the pursuit of perfection. You might become discouraged if your affiliate site isn't instantly a hit or if your content isn't viral worthy right away. But here's a nugget of wisdom: even the most successful entrepreneurs began with content that would make them cringe today. They learned; they adjusted. They understood that imperfect action beats inaction every time. Aim for progress, not perfection.

Another common pitfall? Choosing the wrong products to promote. It's easy to be swayed by high commission rates or trendy items, but if they don't align with your audience's interests or values, you're swimming against the tide. Be discerning. Nurture trust by recommending products you believe in and that provide real value to your followers. This will create a foundation of authenticity that can weather any storm.

Now, let's tackle something that can grip even the most zealous entrepreneur: burnout. When you're managing a side hustle alongside life's other commitments, the candle can start burning at both ends quickly. Be smart about your time. Incorporate tools that automate repetitive tasks and delegate when possible. And please, take a break. Your health and creativity require recharge time to thrive.

On the technical front, don't let SEO intimidate you. Yes, it's complex, and yes, search engine algorithms seem to flip-flop more than a politician in election season. But here's the kicker – you don't need to be an SEO guru to get results. Focus on fundamental principles like keyword research and quality content. Keep abreast of major changes, sure, but don't let the minutiae bog you down. Excellence in a few areas trumps mediocrity across the board.

Monetization is also a slippery slope. Too many ads or overly aggressive selling can repel visitors faster than you can say 'bounce rate'. Strike a healthy balance. Your audience is there for insight, not a hard sell. Let monetization be a function of your value proposition, not vice versa.

Let's also not forget one of the great ironies – the paralysis by analysis. With the abundance of data available to you, it's easy to drown in the details. Metrics and analytics are powerful, but they're also a bit like quicksand. Stay grounded by focusing on a few key performance indicators that align with your goals. Otherwise, you'll be swamped with graphs and figures that detract from real, revenue-generating work.

One pitfall that can creep up unnoticed is the echo chamber effect. It's natural to seek advice from like-minded individuals, but too much harmony can lead to stagnation. Cultivate a diverse network of connections; be open to fresh perspectives and constructive criticism. These might be the catalyst for the innovative breakthrough you've been waiting for.

Similar lines don't fall victim to imposter syndrome. Feeling like a fraud can quash your entrepreneurial spirit. Remember, ability isn't about knowing everything – it's about knowing where to find solutions and how to apply them. Own your strengths, focus on continuous learning, and squash those self-defeating thoughts under the heft of your accomplishments, no matter how small they may seem.

Now, have you considered the legal maze? Copyrights, trademarks, disclaimers – oh my. It's a lot to digest, but it's non-negotiable. Protect yourself by understanding at least the basics of the legalities involved. There are resources to guide you, and it's worth the effort to avoid the potential catastrophes of infringement or other legal woes.

A word on diversification: don't put all your eggs in one affiliate program basket. Platforms change policies; markets evolve. If your entire income streams from only one source, you're one policy update away from disaster. Expand your portfolio with assorted products and affiliate systems to buffer against unexpected shocks.

Digital presence is another mighty pitfall. Maybe you've been focusing all your energies on your blog, leaving social media in the dust. Or vice versa. An integrated approach is key. Not all platforms will be right for you, but you can't afford to ignore them altogether. Find the ones where your audience hangs out, and make yourself at home there, too.

Remember that growth takes time. It's easy to feel discouraged when you compare your start to someone else's middle. But consider this: the only fair comparison is where you are today to where you were yesterday. Celebrate those tiny victories relentlessly. They accumulate and eventually compound into strides you can be proud of.

Customer service might not be the first thing you think of when it comes to affiliate marketing but neglect it at your peril. If a customer has a poor experience with a product you recommended, it reflects on you. Be proactive. Follow up. Address issues quickly and keep a transparent line of communication. Satisfaction is contagious, and delighted customers are your best advocates.

Finally, remember why you started. There will be days when motivation is in short supply. Go back to your why. Your passion is the engine of your enterprise. Feed it with your goals and dreams, and let that drive push you through the obstacles you'll inevitably encounter.

As you gingerly navigate these common pitfalls, stay flexible and stay persistent. Adaptability is the hallmark of an entrepreneur who can ride the waves of change to shore. With a vigilant mindset and a toolkit of strategies from this road map, your journey to financial freedom has the potential to be not just successful, but also truly gratifying.

Adapting and Pivoting Your Strategy

In the entrepreneurial tapestry, adapting and pivoting aren't just buzzwords, they're lifelines. Accept it: what worked yesterday might not work tomorrow. Markets evolve, technology leaps forward, and your audience's preferences change like the wind. To keep your passive income streams gushing, you must refine the fine art of adaptation and stay limber for the inevitable pivot. Remember, your strategy isn't carved in stone—it's sketched in the sand, ready to be reshaped by the tide of change.

Consider your affiliate marketing venture. It's a dynamic beast, thriving on the fresh and the innovative. When a product you're promoting suddenly drops in popularity or the company you've partnered with changes its policies, what's your game plan? You'll need to scour the horizon for new opportunities, replacing what's not working with products that have the potential to scale.

Keep an eye on your metrics. They're the compass that guides your business. If conversion rates start to dip or traffic begins to wane, don't wait for a storm. Dive deep into analytics to understand why. Is your SEO no longer effective? Are people not engaging with your emails? Understanding the 'why' behind the numbers powers smart decisions and propels swift action.

Network with other affiliate marketers. They're a goldmine of insights and experiences. They can offer you fresh perspectives or even partner with you to use mutual strengths. Moreover, stay glued to industry trends and customer feedback. If there's a shift toward a new type of service or product, you've got to be at the forefront, introducing it to your followers before anyone else does.

Flexibility is your best friend. It allows you to react quickly and reframe your failures as learning opportunities. Ever tried promoting a product that just didn't resonate with your audience? It's tough, but rather than lick your wounds, use it as a chance to dig deeper. Maybe you need a different approach to communication, or perhaps it's time to redefine your target audience.

What if the platform you've sworn by isn't delivering results anymore? It's aggravating, but it's not the end. Pivoting might mean hopping onto newer platforms where your audience has migrated. It's about staying relevant and visible where your customers are, even if it means leaving your comfort zone.

Innovation is your wild card. Don't shy away from experimenting with new types of content or marketing strategies. Short video content, for instance, has exploded recently. If you aren't leveraging that in your content strategy, you might be missing out on huge engagement opportunities. Remember, each platform has its norms, experiment within those boundaries to find what resonates with your audience.

The most successful entrepreneurs keep their fingers on the pulse of their business. If you're not dialed into every twitch and beep of your operation, you're flying blind. Stay on top of industry news, subscribe to thought leaders in your niche, and never stop learning. Your adaptability quotient directly correlates with your knowledge depth.

Financial backing can't be overlooked either. It's critical to manage your cash flow carefully to ensure you've got the muscle to pivot when needed. This might mean saving a part of your passive income for reinvestment or having a diversified portfolio that can cushion you against any single income stream drying up.

During a pivot, communication is key. Your audience should never feel abandoned or confused during your transition phase. Be transparent about changes and updates, and always highlight the benefits that these new directions promise. It's not just about changing lanes; it's about taking your audience on a joyful ride to a better destination.

Always remember, pivoting doesn't mean throwing everything out the window. It's about strategic shifts – leveraging the pieces that work and discarding those that don't. The core of your brand and the trust you've built remain unchanged. The pivot is just recalibrating your compass to make sure you're headed towards success.

The fear of failure can be paralyzing. But in the grand tapestry of entrepreneurship, it's nothing but a stitch in a much larger pattern. Embrace the notion that failure is integral to success, it is a catalyst for change. Every misstep is a lesson, and every setback is a setup for a comeback – provided you're willing to adapt and pivot your strategy with grace and determination.

And finally, celebrate every small win on your journey. These triumphs, no matter how trivial they might seem, are the steppingstones towards significant breakthroughs. They build momentum, morale, and reaffirm that you're moving in the right direction.

Tying it all together, the willingness to adapt and the courage to pivot are what separate the thriving passive income entrepreneurs from the crowd. It's a bold blend of resilience, foresight, and relentless innovation. Keep your strategy fluid, your outlook optimistic, and your actions deliberate. Your passive income dreams are not just a possibility but an inevitability, so long as you're prepared to navigate each twist and turn on the road to financial freedom.

As we wrap up this section on adapting and pivoting, keep your sight set on the bigger picture. Stay curious, remain vigilant, and always be ready to steer your ship to the most promising waters, even if that means charting a course you've never sailed before. Your nimbleness in strategy will be the wind in your sails, propelling you ever forward to the horizon of success.

Chapter 8

Your Roadmap to Financial Freedom

As we pull into the destination of our journey together, it's essential to reflect on the vibrant landscape of opportunities that lies before you. We've voyaged through the intricate mechanics of passive income and the labyrinths of affiliate marketing, delved into the artistry of content creation, amplified our digital echoes across the vast online universe, engaged with dynamic communities, scaled the peaks of automation, and charted a course around daunting obstacles. Now, at the summit of our exploration, a promising vista extends—your roadmap to financial freedom.

The pathway you've embarked upon isn't for the faint of heart, but then again, neither are you. Entrepreneurs, bloggers, and side hustlers alike share the thrilling quest for autonomy and financial liberation. The strategies and insights gathered here serve as your compass, pointing to fertile valleys where passive income streams can flourish.

Let's crystallize the vision: financial freedom isn't a dream beyond reach; it's a tangible reality meticulously constructed by your hands, one intentional brick at a time. Remember that each stream of income you develop acts as a tributary, ultimately merging into a powerful river that can sustain you indefinitely.

Your efforts in laying the foundation of passive income are akin to planting a garden. Each strategy you've learned is a seed with potential for abundant growth. Cultivating these seeds requires patience, perseverance, and a keen sense of timing, but the harvest—your financial freedom—is worth every drop of sweat and every moment spent tilling the soil.

In your affiliate marketing ventures, you've gained the blueprint for an ecosystem where partnerships and products synergize, creating a structure that supports your growth and sustains your successes. As you continue to choose your collaborators with discernment and align your offerings with the market's pulse, your financial tapestry will become ever more intricate and resilient.

Content creation, the beating heart of your online persona, is where your unique voice resonates, engaging and enchanting your audience. Whether through blog posts that awaken curiosity or social media blasts that capture the zeitgeist, your content is the siren song that beckons traffic to your digital shores, converting passersby into loyal patrons.

The expanse of the internet is your playground, and your online presence is your fortress. Bolster it with the blogging strategies and social media tactics you've honed. Nurture your digital garden, and watch as it yields a cornucopia of traffic, leads, and, ultimately, revenue. Tend to your fortress, and like any stronghold, it will stand the tests of time and change.

Evolving with your audience is the dance of growth. Your email marketing finesse and community-building acumen are the steps to this dance. Lead with value and follow with engagement, continuously cementing the bond between you and your audience. This bond is the lifeline of your business, pulsating with loyalty and replenished by a stream of passive income.

Embracing automation and scaling bridges the chasm between striving and thriving. Tools and technologies are the allies waiting to shoulder some of your burdens, freeing you to ascend towards broader horizons and bolder aims. Utilize them to transform your operations from reactive to proactive, and your empire will expand beyond what manual effort could ever achieve.

Inevitably, challenges will appear, as they do on any worthwhile adventure. However, your newfound resilience and strategic agility make you well-equipped to navigate these trials. The common pitfalls that once seemed insurmountable are now mere stepping stones on your path to victory.

Your roadmap is not a straight line, nor should it be. Financial freedom is discovered in the flexibility to adapt, the creativity to innovate, and the wisdom to pivot when the landscape demands it. Keep your goal in focus but allow the path itself to be fluid.

While this book may signal a pause in our direct dialogue, it's far from the end of your journey. Consider it rather as a launchpad for the multitude of endeavors that await you. Arm yourself with the added resources, checklists, and templates found in the appendices; they are designed to keep your trajectory true and your momentum steadfast.

As you advance from here, carry with you the spirit of empowerment that has been instilled within these pages. Your route to financial freedom is personal and unique, paved with your aspirations, defined by your choices, and carved out through your actions. In your hands lies the power to manifest the liberty and prosperity that you look for.

You stand at the threshold of limitless potential, gazing upon the horizon of what can be. Forge ahead with courage, with determination, and with the knowledge that each step on this roadmap brings you closer to the life of abundance and autonomy you envision. Financial freedom is not a distant dream; it's a reality waiting to be claimed.

So go forth, carry the torch of entrepreneurship with pride, and illuminate the path for others to follow. With each milestone you reach, remember that this roadmap isn't just a guide; it's a testament to your resolve and a beacon for your unwavering pursuit of financial freedom. The journey continues, and the world awaits the unique imprint of your success.

Appendix A

And here you are, standing at the threshold of a new chapter in your entrepreneurial journey, armed with the insights and strategies that can turn the dream of a consistent passive income stream into your everyday reality. But remember, the landscape of affiliate marketing and digital entrepreneurship is ever-evolving — it's a vast ocean of opportunity that demands continuous navigation.

Additional Resources for Continuous Learning

As someone who's poised to make their mark on the digital landscape, know that learning never really stops. It's vital to stay ahead of the curve, to be in the know, and to constantly fill your toolkit with fresh ideas and cutting-edge tricks of the trade. To aid you in this quest, we've compiled a curated list of additional resources to help you keep that edge:

- **Industry Blogs:** Stay updated with the latest trends and best practices.
- **Podcasts:** Tune into the minds of successful entrepreneurs and marketing mavens.
- **Online Courses:** Sharpen your skills with courses from reputable platforms.
- **Webinars and Live Streams:** Engage with experts in real-time and ask critical issues.
- **Networking Events:** Build relationships that could open doors to new opportunities.
- **Books:** Dive into comprehensive guides by thought leaders and trailblazers.

- Immersing yourself in these resources can be as energizing as it is enlightening, injecting new life into your projects whenever you hit a plateau or need a fresh perspective.

Checklists and Templates for Your Affiliate Journey

Now, let's not just throw you into the deep end without a lifeline. To ensure you're never adrift, Appendix A also provides you with practical checklists and templates designed to streamline your workflow and keep you organized:

- **Startup Checklist:** A step-by-step rundown to set up your affiliate business.
- **Content Calendar Template:** Plan your blogging and social media schedule like a pro.
- **Email Campaign Planner:** Craft and track your email marketing efforts with precision.
- **SEO Checklist:** Ensure every piece of content is perfected for maximum reach.
- **Performance Tracker:** Keep tabs on your progress and find areas for improvement.
- Embrace these tools to sharpen your focus and execute your strategies with unerring precision. You'll find that having a clear structure for your day-to-day tasks not only enhances your productivity but also gives you a sense of control and calm amidst the hustle.
- Take what you've learned throughout this book and combine it with the resources and tools found in this Appendix. Know that your path won't always be smooth — there will be bumps and detours. Yet, with resilience, a thirst for knowledge, and a solid plan of action, you can and will carve out your niche in the world of affiliate marketing.

- Empower yourself each day, because in this dynamic digital era, the potential to craft a fulfilling and profitable online business is truly limitless. So go ahead, take that leap, and keep pushing the boundaries. Your version of success is out there, waiting for you to seize it.

Additional Resources for Continuous Learning Building a passive income empire isn't a one-time event; it's a continuous journey filled with learning and growth. To truly excel in this arena, it's pivotal to keep abreast of new strategies, tools, and trends. In this section, we'll explore a variety of resources that can serve as your companions in the lifelong quest for knowledge and professional development.

Every entrepreneur knows that the landscape of business is ever-changing. Books are timeless classics in learning, and they provide in-depth knowledge on subjects ranging from marketing strategies to personal development. Make it a habit to read regularly, focusing on recent publications to keep your strategies fresh and relevant. For starters, consider a mix of timeless entrepreneurial bibles and up-to-date thought leadership pieces that delve into the digital economy.

Podcasts are another goldmine for entrepreneurs. They allow you to learn from experts and fellow entrepreneurs while you're on the go. Subscribe to podcasts focusing on entrepreneurship, digital marketing, and passive income. Take advantage of your daily commute, workout, or any routine task by soaking in new insights and stories from those who have been there and done that.

Online courses and webinars are fantastic for structured learning. Platforms such as **Coursera, Udemy**, and **Skillshare** offer a wealth of courses taught by industry experts. These resources provide the benefit of pacing your learning and often offer interactive components like forums and projects. Keep an eye out for courses that offer certification as a bonus to your resume.

Blogging is still an integral part of continuous learning. By following influential bloggers in the affiliate marketing and entrepreneurship space, you can access a steady stream of insights and experiences. Plus, engaging with blogger communities can bring about opportunities for collaboration and mentorship.

Networking events and conferences are irreplaceable resources for continuous learning. They provide a platform for meeting peers, sharing knowledge, and discovering up-and-coming innovations. Make a point of attending relevant events to remain connected and informed. Remember, the relationships you forge can become invaluable sources of knowledge and aid.

Don't overlook the importance of social media as a learning tool. LinkedIn, Twitter, and even Instagram can provide abundant information from thought leaders and practitioners. Follow hashtags relevant to your industry, engage with content creators, and don't hesitate to enter the conversation yourself.

Industry reports and case studies present a more analytical approach to learning. Keeping up with industry research can help you understand market trends and consumer behavior. This data-driven lens can sharpen your decision-making and help expect shifts in your business environment.

Workshops and boot camps provide an immersive learning experience, often focusing on hands-on skills and practical knowledge. These are invaluable for entrepreneurs who receive help from a more tactile approach to learning and enjoy the camaraderie of group learning environments.

Mastermind groups gather like-minded individuals who are interested in mutual growth. By joining or forming a mastermind, you can receive help from the collective wisdom of the group, holding each other accountable and pushing towards your goals with shared enthusiasm.

Mentorship is perhaps one of the most direct ways to facilitate continuous learning. A mentor who has navigated the terrain of passive income can offer personalized advice and guidance. Consider seeking out a mentorship relationship, whether informally or through organizations that pair experienced entrepreneurs with newcomers.

Trade publications and news sites should become staples in your daily reading routine. Keeping informed about the economic environment, technological advances, and regulatory changes can help you stay ahead of the curve and adjust your strategies, as necessary.

For those who prefer a more academic approach, research journals and publications in the fields of business and marketing provide peer-reviewed studies and findings. They can be dense, but the insights gleaned from academic research can introduce you to cutting-edge concepts and methodologies.

Always remember to reflect on and analyze your own experiences. Keeping a journal or blog about your personal business journey allows you to track your progress, reflect on successes and challenges, and share your learning with others. This reflective practice is a cornerstone of continuous personal growth.

Finally, consider teaching or consulting in your area of expertise. One of the best ways to solidify your knowledge is to teach it to others. Whether through creating online courses or offering consultancy services, sharing your ability can deepen your understanding and provide another stream of passive income.

Continuous learning is your secret weapon in the dynamic world of passive income. By using these added resources, you stay skilled, nimble, and mentally prepared for whatever your entrepreneurial journey throws your way. Embrace the habit of lifelong learning and watch as each new piece of knowledge propels you closer to your goals of financial freedom and success.